Our Pets

Birds

by Lisa J. Amstutz

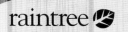
raintree
a Capstone company — publishers for children

Raintree is an imprint of Capstone Global Library Limited, a company incorporated in England and Wales having its registered office at 264 Banbury Road, Oxford, OX2 7DY – Registered company number: 6695582

www.raintree.co.uk
myorders@raintree.co.uk

Text © Capstone Global Library Limited 2018
The moral rights of the proprietor have been asserted.

Edited by Marissa Kirkman
Designed by Juliette Peters (cover) and Charmaine Whitman (interior)
Picture research by Morgan Walters
Production by Laura Manthe
Originated by Capstone Global Library Limited
Printed and bound in India

ISBN 978 1 4747 5716 4
21 20 19 18 17
10 9 8 7 6 5 4 3 2 1

British Library Cataloguing in Publication Data
A full catalogue record for this book is available from the British Library.

Acknowledgements
We would like to thank the following for permission to reproduce photographs: Dreamstime: Suksao, bottom 9; Shutterstock: cynoclub, back cover, DarAnna, 19, Elena Abduramanova, bottom 7, glen gaffney, top 21, Imran Ashraf, top 7, Morgan Rauscher, bottom 21, Mr Aesthetics, (wood) design element throughout, Nipa Noymol, 11, PrakapenkaAlena, Cover, ShutterstockProfessional, 1, small1, 13, varis kusujarit, 5, YK, top 9, 15, 17

Every effort has been made to contact copyright holders of material reproduced in this book. Any omissions will be rectified in subsequent printings if notice is given to the publisher.

All the Internet addresses (URLs) given in this book were valid at the time of going to press. However, due to the dynamic nature of the Internet, some addresses may have changed, or sites may have changed or ceased to exist since publication. While the author and publisher regret any inconvenience this may cause readers, no responsibility for any such changes can be accepted by either the author or the publisher.

Contents

Listen!

Tweet, tweet!

A bird hops onto its perch.

It sings a pretty song.

Birds make many sounds.

They sing. They chatter.

They screech.

Sounds can show how

birds feel.

All about birds

Pet birds can be big or small.

They can be many colours.

Some birds have crests
on their heads.

Peck! Birds use their beaks to eat food.

Birds eat seeds and nuts.

They eat fruits and vegetables too.

Birds clean their feathers.

They use their beaks.

This is called preening.

Growing up

Pet birds lay eggs in a nest box.

The mother sits on the eggs.

She keeps them warm.

Look! The eggs hatched.

The mother cares

for her chicks.

She brings them food.

Fun pets

Birds are fun pets.

They play with toys.

Turn on music.

They might dance!

Birds can learn tricks.

Some can even learn to talk.

Hello!

Glossary

beak hard front part of the mouth of a bird

chick baby bird

crest tuft of feathers on a bird's head

feather one of the flat, light parts that grow from the bird's skin and cover its body; feathers help birds fly

hatch to break out of an egg

nest place where birds lay eggs and bring up young

perch support, such as a peg, on which a bird rests

preen to clean and arrange feathers; a bird preens its feathers with its beak

Read more

Beaky's Guide to Caring for Your Bird (Pets' Guides), Isabel Thomas (Raintree, 2016)

Little Kids First Big Book of Birds, Catherine D. Hughes (National Geographic Kids, 2016)

Pet Birds: Questions and Answers (Pet Questions and Answers), Christina Mia Gardeski (Capstone Press, 2017)

Websites

www.bbc.co.uk/cbeebies/topics/pets
Discover a variety of pets, play pet games and watch pet videos on this fun BBC website.

www.bluecross.org.uk
Find out more about how to choose a pet and care for your pet on the Blue Cross website.

Comprehension questions

1. What do pet birds eat?

2. Where do pet birds lay eggs?

3. Would you like to own a pet bird? Why or why not?

Index